SHAPES AND PEOPLE

FOR SOPHIE, HER NIECE
AND HER NEPHEW

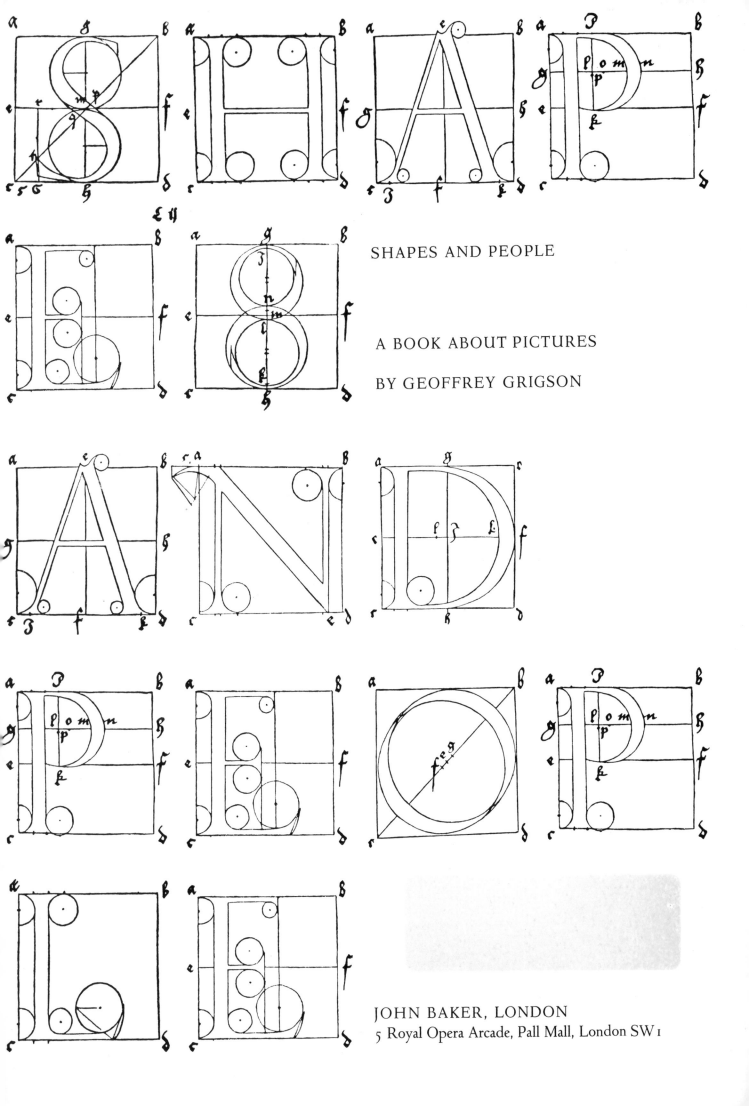

SHAPES AND PEOPLE

A BOOK ABOUT PICTURES

BY GEOFFREY GRIGSON

JOHN BAKER, LONDON
5 Royal Opera Arcade, Pall Mall, London SW1

DESIGNED AND PRODUCED BY BANKS AND MILES
7a GRAFTON STREET, LONDON W1

SBN 212 98354 7
The letters on the title page are from an alphabet
designed by Dürer.

© 1969 by Geoffrey Grigson
First published 1969
by John Baker Publishers Limited
5 Royal Opera Arcade, Pall Mall, London SW1
All rights reserved
Printed at The Curwen Press, London E13, England

# THE PICTURES, THE ARTISTS AND THE QUOTATIONS

*Large capitals indicate the pictures in colour*

WHERE THE QUOTATIONS COME FROM

have a long look at your head, face forward, in a looking-glass. If you can draw, try drawing your mirror-image (which will be the wrong way round, your left ear will become your right ear, but never mind): it will tell you something about pictures. Your face on the paper will be made up of lines – which you found in the mirror. The lines define shapes, all put together the shapes make the drawing. You can add colour. Lines, shapes, colours make the picture of YOURSELF.

Let's forget that a moment, let's forget that *you*, and declare: The picture is simply – ITSELF.

A great artist (a painting by him comes on page 27, with information about him above it) pronounced that a picture is 'an original combination of lines and colours that set one another off'.

Only lines and colours (I shall change it to lines, shapes and colours): that is all: nothing about whether it shows a cat or a catherine wheel. Cat or catherine wheel, yak or you, it will still be lines, shapes, colours – ITSELF.

And *you* as well, after all.

Between paper and mirror you exclaim 'Do I look like that?' 'Is that me?' 'What is *me*?' Which last is a very large question. Since people interest people (What's he like? Is she nice? I can't stand him), it follows that people shaped into pictures by artists are likely to include individuals, or the faces of individuals – perhaps with neck, shoulders, or body – the face being the part which seems to reveal what we are.

Someone may want himself painted, to tell others now or in a hundred years what he looks like. The artist may enjoy painting him because the lines, shapes and colours of the particular face attract him (on top of which the face's owner may pay him for the job). So in this book I begin with PORTRAITS – and since an artist may like to tell himself or others about his own looks or his nature, I shall begin with some artists by artists, some SELF-PORTRAITS coming back later to other portraits.

When Henri Rousseau painted Henri Rousseau (opposite) I wouldn't say he was puzzled by himself. He was announcing – because he was a humble man who found himself in middle age among artists, after being an excise-man most of his life – 'I am Henri Rousseau, I am a Parisian like other artists, I have a beard like other artists. Serious, dignified, I am standing by the Seine; there's the Eiffel Tower.'

Of course he was a real artist. Of course as he painted clouds, balloon, coloured sun, coloured air, leaves, and flags, his announcement *This is me, the artist Rousseau* mattered less to him than assembling lines and colours. A living French poet says that Rousseau wanted to show us what he saw, and that what he saw was loved. He loved everything.

Turn him upside down: on his palette you will find two names – of the two women he loved most, Clémence, his dead wife, who had given him 9 children; Joséphine, who was to be his second wife. It is as if he dipped his brush, when he painted, into his love for Clémence and Joséphine. A poem about Rousseau by one of his friends says that an angel and a bird on the angel's shoulder sang together in praise of Rousseau, and that Rousseau *was* both the bird and the angel, and that Rousseau also carved those two adored names together on a public bench in Paris.

'That's me, and that's you', Pieter Bruegel seems to say in this drawing, 'I'm an artist, you're a patron. I may look queer and old-fashioned; but you don't look very bright yourself, or very up-to-date. And you don't know anything about pictures. I don't need glasses to see what I see. As a matter of fact I'm looking at the world and not at my picture, and I see the world is about as queer as I am; and there are you, Mr Chairman of the National Gallery, with your glasses on your pokey nose and your eyes half-shut, and you pretend to see my picture, and you see exactly nothing, nothing. At least I'm painting, I have a brush in my hand. You've got your hand on your purse (don't let the money fall out). You're idle, and money is all you care about.

My mouth may be turned down, but as I say, it's a queer world I see and put in my pictures, and you have thin lips, and you don't care about the world, only yourself and the stock market. Yes, I'm dirty and hairy and not so young, you're old and dry and have no eyebrows. Still, we're in the same drawing, we're part of the same world, painter, and fraud; perhaps two frauds.'

(All the same, don't forget, when you look at this drawing which Pieter Bruegel made of himself and the patron of art, about 1565, that a drawing is *an original assembly of lines*.)

10

I am not sure Hokusai, great Japanese master, isn't saying something similar in the lines of his drawing of himself, as an old, old man. He is 83 (Bruegel was about half as old in his self-portrait): he is wrinkled, bald, skinny. 'I've seen the world, enjoyed it, can make jokes about it, about you, about me. And I can still draw, I can still draw. What can you do?'

Artists can make us feel humble, by pictures or drawings, without themselves acting in a superior way.

There is more of Bruegel to come later in this book; and of Hokusai—whom you will see, to go on with, over the page in another drawing, looking older still, and weaker, and more serious. In the Hokusai over the page the lines match the different feeling (of course, again, the lines *are* the feeling), they go in a slower, more solemn way, downwards. In the Hokusai on this page the lines jump about almost skittishly; in the drawing on the next page they flow and fall like some of the solemn waterfalls Hokusai had walked to in the Japanese mountains and made drawings of when he was young and strong.

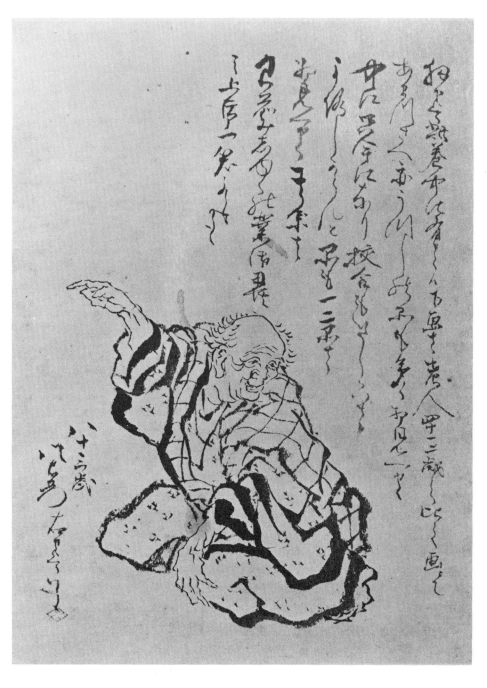

SELF-PORTRAIT
Katsushika Hokusai (1760 – 1849)

SELF-PORTRAIT
Katsushika Hokusai
(1760–1849)

Leonardo da Vinci, by himself, in a grand assembly of lines, old, with rippling hair, mouth turned down a little, eyes seeming to look out of him into everything he had discovered and felt; not happy, but not dismayed altogether by world, man, life and time.

We think of him as one of the greatest of all our race of men.

Turn back to page 10: doesn't he have rather the same look in his face, his mouth, his eyes, his intentness, as Bruegel? Only, the great Bruegel had more of a fantastic person inside him, as well as a serious one. He drew himself with his hair pushing out under his cap like uncombed roots. Leonardo's hair and beard ripple down in great dignity: he makes himself look like one of our great discoverers, like someone who knows human nobility and smallness, someone who knows very well that he is a master of what we call the Renaissance, the time of universal discovery and new feelings. When I look at the two drawings I ask myself 'Could Bruegel have seen Leonardo's Leonardo – drawn about 50 years before Bruegel's Bruegel – and then made *his* version of it, to fit his own northern queerness?' As if he had said 'Grand fellow, but can't stand all that Italian swank'?

The swank was justified. In the year of this drawing, about 1516, I would say, Leonardo da Vinci (he had been born at Vinci, not far from Florence, in 1452) was some 64 years old. He had been everything, painter, sculptor, architect, engineer, inventor. Living now in France as 'first painter, engineer and architect to the king', he had spent a life investigating nature from leaves to mountains. Like a modern scientist he had written down 'All our knowledge has its origin in our perceptions'. He had been asking questions all his life, and finding answers. He had earned that grand look.

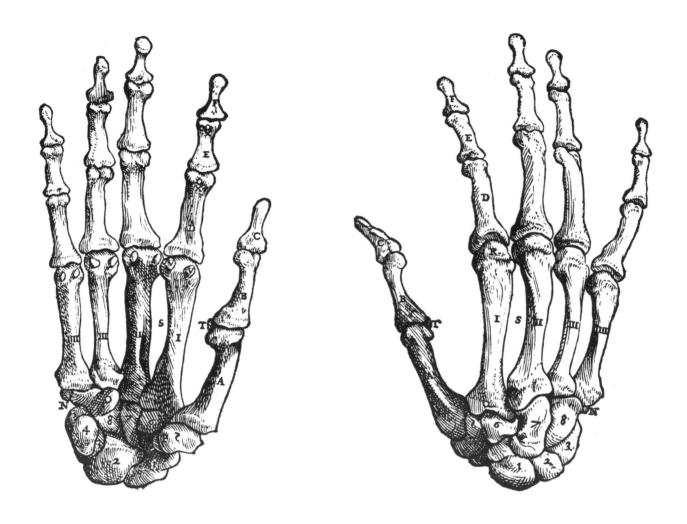

Leonardo was one of the men who dissected human bodies, in order to learn the mechanism of man. Another was Titian—born about 35 years later than Leonardo—who lived, the great master painter of Venice, richest city then in the world, until he was ninety, or perhaps more than ninety. Probably it was Titian who made drawings of our inside structure which were engraved for the first sublime book of the science of anatomy ('anatomy' comes from a Greek word which means a 'cutting up'), written by Andreas Vesalius of Brussels. It was called *De Humani Corporis Fabrica*—'About the Fabric of Man's Body', and was published in 1543 (Leonardo, by then, had been dead 24 years).

Above, from this book which was as much a voyage of discovery as going from our Europe for the first time to America or India, you see the bones of your left hand, palm upwards, then back upwards, and how they fit together. On the right, you see a strange view of your spinal nerves.

Men stripped to their bones—to their skeletons; to their muscles, to their veins, to their arteries, or like this to their nerves, walk upright through the book with a mournful dignity, 'We are dead, we have been dissected, we are all mortal, we are sad. But look how wonderfully, how perfectly we are made.'

Engravings from DE HUMANI CORPORIS FABRICA, 1543

TRIGINTA PARI-  VM NERVORVM
*QVAE A' DORSALI ME*  *DVLLA DORSI OSSIBVS*
*contenta originem ducunt, nuda delineatio*  *ea proportione expressa, qua superiùs ue-*
*næ cauæ & magnæ arteriæ delineationes*  *exhibuimus. Hæc trium subsequentibus*
*Capitibus communium figura-*  *rum secunda numeratur.*

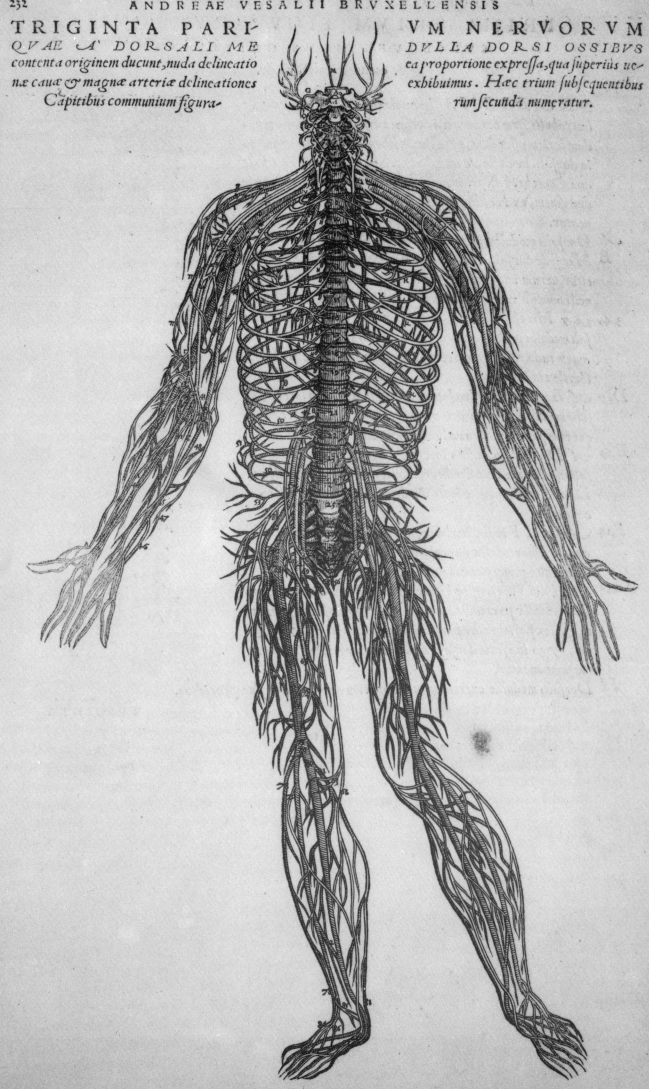

Poets, as well as great exploring artists, great exploring doctors, like Vesalius,
felt man in these times as both a wonder and a mortal thing. They wrote poems
or plays for which these engraved men of bones, muscles, veins, arteries and
nerves would do as illustrations. Remember Shakespeare's Hamlet (who was
soon picking up skulls in the churchyard) talking about the wonder of man, who
all the same is dust (look it up, *Hamlet*, Act 2, Scene 2, Hamlet talking prose,
not poetry). For a change here is another poet, Sir John Davies, five years
younger than Shakespeare, in a poem which appeared almost at the same time as
*Hamlet*, at the end of the century which had been distinguished by Leonardo,
Titian and Vesalius:

*I know my body's of so frail a kind*
    *As force without, fevers within, can kill;*
*I know the heavenly nature of my mind,*
    *But 'tis corrupted both in wit and will;*

*I know my soul has power to know all things,*
    *Yet is she blind and ignorant in all;*
*I know I am one of nature's little kings,*
    *Yet to the least and vilest things am thrall.*

*I know my life's a pain and but a span,*
    *I know my sense is mocked with everything;*
*And to conclude, I know myself a man,*
    *Which is a proud and yet a wretched thing.*

Leonardo said that a good painter had two chief objects to paint. One was
man, the other was 'the intention of his soul', or as we might say, a man and his
character or his personality. Painting the 'soul', a difficult job, meant painting
the way a man indicated it by his looks and by his movements. Leonardo there-
fore gave plenty of time to watching movement, and expression—men frowning,
smiling, laughing, sneezing, yawning. The drawing on the right isn't by him,
but by a follower (perhaps—see page 26—by Bernardino Luini). I'd say the man
is just going to sneeze, shutting his eyes in that blind moment which comes with
sneezing, and pulling his mouth in. A friend of mine won't have that, and says
the man has just smelt rather a nasty smell—though he is good-humoured about
the smell and not upset. I prefer the sneeze explanation. Ask someone to pretend
to sneeze, and see for yourself.

No one thinks about angels sneezing or wearing personal expressions. Here I have set a row of singing angels next to a pop group, solemn figures next to everyday figures. The angels come from a great picture by Piero della Francesca, who was born thirty or forty years before Leonardo and wasn't so interested in personality. Lorenzo Costa, who painted this pop group, was much the same age as Leonardo, and I would say that his singers, decidedly, are persons or individuals, even if it is unfair to compare angels down from heaven with a trio of earthly musicians.

Piero made his figures—usually out of the Bible, or saints—very still, solemn and solid. But both painters assemble shape against shape. You can learn the pleasure of the rhythm in shapes if you run your eye along the mouths of these happy yet solemn angels and these three ordinary people, from left to right. The angel mouths—nearly closed, more open, nearly closed, wide open, nearly closed again—are like music; the only sound, almost the only movement in stillness. With his mouths Lorenzo Costa tries the same thing but doesn't manage it so well. Or run your eye along the openings below each neck, angels and trio. Each opening is a little different, together they make bars of the music of shape.

THE NATIVITY (detail)
Piero della Francesca
(1410/20 – 1492)

THE CONCERT
Lorenzo Costa (*c* 1460 – 1535)

Are painters odd people? Often they are not happy unless they are painting; which means they have no time for anything else; which means they have no time for business or social life; which means – to sociable, businesslike people – that they seem eccentric. Whereas the great artists are generally as 'respectable' as anyone else. But not always. Adriaen Brouwer lived among the fuddled riffraff of the Netherlands, who drank themselves silly or drugged themselves silly with strong doped tobacco, which helped them through their degeneracy, but only made them still more degenerate.

But see what a painter he was, in between; painting this sodden world, watching grey smoke curl out of the drunk's red wet lips, watching a rough dentist extracting rotten teeth from another rough customer. He soon died. He spent money as he came by it, he passed some time in prison, then caught the plague at Antwerp, when he was about 32.

Other great artists cared for Brouwer's pictures without caring whether he was nice to know or not. Rubens and Rembrandt owned pictures by him; and Rubens, courtly painter and diplomat, had Brouwer taken out of his poor grave and buried with honour in a fine church – where the company wouldn't have pleased him at all when he was alive. He lived from picture to picture. One story about him is that if a picture didn't sell, he would burn it and paint one which seemed likelier to pay for his girls and his drinks.

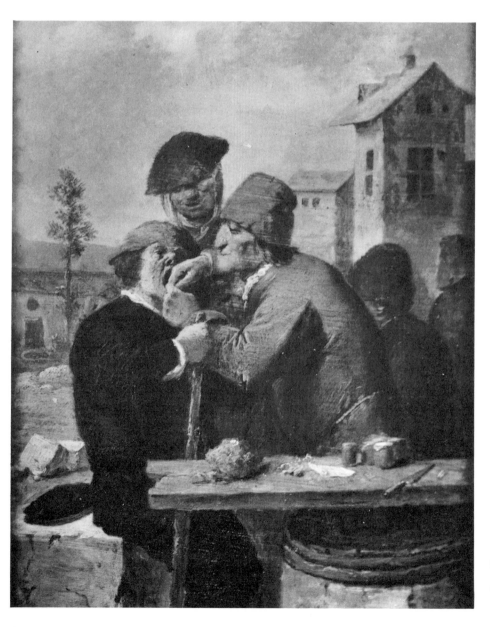

VILLAGE DENTISTRY
Adriaen Brouwer (1605/6 – 1638)

THE BEEKEEPERS
Pieter Bruegel (c1525/30–1569)

Have you noticed, not just how strange people can look, but how they can look like birds or insects or fruit or something inhumanly queer on two legs?

We are intrigued when it happens in fact, and we like to make it happen in fantasy (which comes from a Greek word meaning a 'making visible'). We wear masks, or make giants walk in a carnival. We know the mask on the man, or the giant in the carnival, isn't real. But that is the pleasure.

Artists are often very good at this kind of 'making visible'. They may be given a clue by some strange look of the ordinary which must have happened often to Pieter Bruegel, grand master of the Netherlands and one of the great magicians of painting, who makes fantasy look real, and the real (like himself and his admirer in the drawing on page 10) look fantastic.

Peasants go and care for their bees and take the honey from the straw skips. They wear baskets on their heads to keep the bees off: Bruegel sees them, he thinks they look like some new race of man, without eyes, mouth or nose. He is fascinated, he draws them, and he makes the drawing illustrate a moral: the boy up the tree is robbing a bird's nest, the grown-ups below rob the nests of the bees: Bruegel writes a proverb in the corner which fits both the boy and the beekeepers: 'He who knows where the nest is knows it, he who robs the nest has it.' But the sight came first, the moral afterwards.

FIDES (detail) Pieter Bruegel

Bruegel does much the same with the people in church, in this part of a drawing which he made to illustrate the virtue of being a true believer. I think he went into a church one day when a friar was up in the pulpit, and was struck by the way all the women with the backs turned to him, with cloaks over their heads, looked different: the friar was preaching to a congregation of ripe pears.

A life of Bruegel written when people could still remember him says he was a quiet and thoughtful man: he didn't say much, but was rather given to scaring friends and pupils with bogey jokes and bogey noises.

People doing things. We stop and watch if we can, if we are not in a hurry, if we are not afraid of being late, if we are not afraid to be idle—and if the things and the people doing them are not hidden away behind a tall hoarding.

In Persia—or Afghanistan—five centuries ago someone who stopped to watch people doing things, without hoardings, without notices saying 'No Admittance', 'Keep Out', 'Private', 'Danger', was, I am certain, Kamal al-Din Bihzad, the greatest of Persian artists. I think he watched masons going up and down ladders, perched on scaffolding, building mosques, castles, tombs, mixing mortar, hauling up materials, cutting the flat tiles which the masons used instead of stone. Then when there was a scene of building a castle to illustrate in a romantic story poem by the Persian poet Nizami (1145–1207), he knew how to manage; and since he was Bihzad, one of the master painters of the world, he knew how to make his masons, all of them as busy as can be, into this delicious pattern of colours. Perhaps 21 masons under a blue sky never wore such colours, green and violet and red and blue and pink and brown and black; but that was art's affair, or Bihzad's affair, the difference between painting and real life. Bihzad painted most of his life in Herat (now in Afghanistan, on the side nearest Persia) which was a great city of the arts under shahs whose ancestor was the conqueror Tamerlane.

In Bihzad's century—putting two castles side by side, from east and from west—a French painter made this other picture of masons at work, for the manuscript, not of a poem, but a serious book on how kings and princes should govern their realms. In his blue robes the King of France comes to see how the masons are getting on, by the riverside, in a scene as gay as Bihzad's.

From *Gouvernment des Rois et des Princes*, French, 15th century

BUILDING THE CASTLE OF
KHAWARNAQ
Kamal al-Din Bihzad
(c1440–c1516)

24

In these two pictures are the people doing something, or being something? Or are they shapes of people, are they lines round people, made into pictures?

Well, the girls are certainly girls, they are certainly bathing and dressing themselves after their dip. Certainly in the other picture there are two laundry women, not just any two women. One is tired, having a good yawn, one is still pressing hard on her iron.

It is really the shapes that mattered to the two painters—most of all the shapes (in each picture there are other shapes as well) of bodies, heads, legs, arms, hands; it is the kind of dance made by these shapes, from left to right and back again (here's an important thing: have you noticed that we look our way into pictures, usually, from left to right? Once we are in, our eyes may be checked, they may go back again, they go up and down and this way and that inside the picture. But the way in is on the left).

These girls were painted on a wall of a rich man's house, in Milan, by Bernardino Luini, whose master was Leonardo da Vinci (page 13). But his pictures tell us he was a very different kind of man. They suggest someone easy-going and gentle, who accepted everything without fuss; which would explain why no one recorded any stories about him. Twenty years after he died, Giorgio Vasari, who put together short lives of the best painters of Italy, could not find much to say about Luini—except that he had lived in Milan, that he had worked in fresco (these girls are in fresco, i.e. they were painted, in thin colour, direct on to plaster while it was still fresh—*fresco* in Italian—and damp). Also he had worked smoothly—just the word—in oils, having been 'an amiable man, liberal in all his actions', and gentle. From his master Leonardo, that grand questioner of life and mind and nature, he had not learned to ask questions or to bother about what Leonardo would have called the soul of someone who was being painted. He had only learned tricks of using his colours and brushes, for the very good pleasure of arranging shapes.

Accordingly he worked out the arrangement of the shapes of these girls who are so gentle, amiable, and charming; especially the one on the far left, bending forward with some of her hair over her back (and see on pages 44 and 45 how Luini painted, in the same house in Milan, Pharaoh's host being overwhelmed by the Red Sea, in the same gentle way, without the anguish of disaster or drowning).

Edgar Degas, three and a half centuries later, in Paris—here was altogether a different man. Yet he would have seen why Luini arranged his girls, his bodies, in that way along the wall, seen from different sides and angles.

Does Degas care about his two laundry women? Not a bit, as human beings. But yes as human bodies. He likes the arrangement of their bodies, heads, arms, elbows, hands, clothes, as they stand side by side. Degas painted ballet-dancers and girls drying after a bath or brushing their hair, caring only for their grace, shape, movement, colours. The same when he pictured race-horses and jockeys, and people at art exhibitions, or sitting in a café. He doesn't bother about their faces, or feelings: catching them as living shapes when they don't know anyone is looking.

Degas was rather a wasp, sharp and sarcastic. He lost his friends, never married, never wanted to, allowing nothing to stop him painting better and better. A picture had to be different from the things apparently assembled in it. So he said 'The air we see in paintings by the old masters isn't the air we breathe.'

Also (remember page 8): 'A picture is an original combination of lines and colours that set one another off'—which covers all painting, very ancient to very 'modern'.

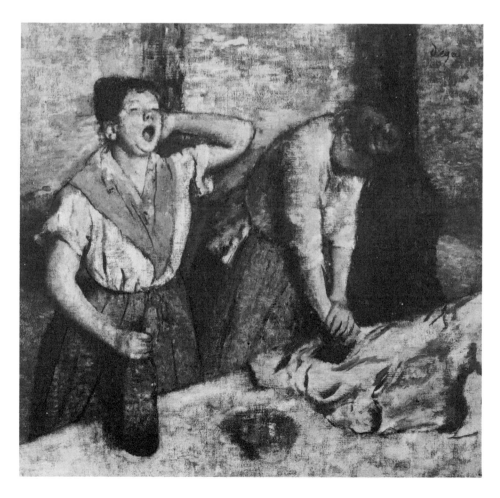

Several pictures so far have been of ordinary people doing ordinary things, instead of special or individual people appearing as their special or individual selves, like Rousseau painting himself beside the Seine, or Bruegel or Hokusai or Leonardo telling us in drawings what they look like. We have had people singing, a dentist pulling a tooth, a smoker smoking, beekeepers beekeeping (even if they were being made to act a proverb), a preacher preaching and a congregation listening, masons building castles in France and Persia, girls bathing, laundry women laundering—or ironing to be exact; after which I ask you to look at these Chinese ladies finishing off new woven silk, painted, or so it is thought, by an emperor.

We shall go on to portraits and stories, to pictures of poets, to journeys and special occasions. A mix-up. But then the point of this book is more to show 'people-pictures', which you may not know and may enjoy, than to be explaining each time what it is that makes art into art. Of course it is artists who make art into art; and artists are simply those who have found they like to draw and paint. They begin: they discover they want to draw and paint again and again, each time differently. A picture-making desire grows inside them, they train their ability to draw lines, they improve their sense of how colours go with each other. They find (if they are lucky, because this does not always happen straightaway) that others as well like the pictures they make.

They go on—sometimes till they cannot hold a brush. Renoir, painter of girls, summer landscape and snow, had brushes tied to his fingers when he was too old and rheumatic to be able to pick up brushes and hold them.

LADIES PREPARING NEWLY WOVEN SILK, details from a scroll attributed to the Emperor Sung Hui-tsung (1082–1135)

It is marvellous and lucky that this ability turns up—in all kinds of human beings, from a saintly friar such as Fra Angelico in Florence in the fifteenth century, to a wild criminal like Caravaggio (pages 46–47) or a lie-about like Adriaen Brouwer (pages 20–21), or an Emperor like Hui-tsung. He ruled in China from 1110 to 1125, an emperor whom his court artists found difficult to serve because of his passion for painting birds on flowering branches: he compelled them to paint pictures as calm and still as his own; and for them it was either obey or be turned out.

In this famous picture the women on the right, pounding the new cloth to make it full and thick, and the women on the left, stretching the cloth, balance an upright movement against a long movement.

The emperor was copying a scroll (which has not survived) by a famous artist Chang Hsüan, who had painted three and a half centuries earlier for the glorious emperor T'ang Hsüan-tsung, one of mankind's supreme encouragers of poetry, painting and music.

29

DUKE HENRY THE PIOUS
Lukas Cranach (1472 – 1553)

Early on, in the truth telling sixteenth century, kings and princes were often less afraid of their own faces – warts, wrinkles and all – when they sat to a painter. But you find a difference in the way two German painters, Albrecht Dürer and Lukas Cranach, in that age of the truth, depict two princes, Frederick the Wise (above) and Henry the Pious (on the left).

A face-picture, a portrait, should tell us what someone is like, yet a good face-picture is one in which the artist is most of all true to himself, or to what happens inside himself to the face he sees. He must let the face work on him without fear, without favour. Both Dürer and Cranach do that. You couldn't call them dishonest painters, who are afraid they won't get portraits to paint unless they make them flattering (most portraits in the Royal Academy every year are products of that kind of cheating).

All the same Dürer and Cranach are true to rather different selves. Dürer painted Frederick the Wise several times, honestly, without cheating; and this independent-minded bachelor prince (who liked truth, good pictures, and good artists) did not mind. In his engraving Dürer concentrates on the strong experienced face, between cap and fur collar, on the old, strong eyes and nose and mouth. Like Leonardo, his senior by nineteen years, Dürer was trying to fix the 'intention of the soul' (page 16) of this prince he knew well, and who had been a good patron to him all his life.

Lukas Cranach (court painter to this same Frederick the Wise of Saxony) was at heart more gay and less inquisitive. He painted some stern portraits in his long life, but in his picture the face of Duke Henry the Pious – if it is there all right, and honestly there – does not seem so very important. It is as if Cranach

31

forgot the princely features for the splendour and gaiety of the princely clothes – this was a marriage picture, the 'hat' the Duke is wearing is made of flowers, of red and white pinks – for the pattern, shapes and lines of the clothes, not overlooking the shapes and lines of the young Duke's hound (the Duke does not have such a defined face as the hound) and the curl of the hound's tail and the curve of the hound's tooth.

PORTRAIT OF A BOY
Bernardino Pintoricchio
(c1454–1513)

Of course a painter could invent a portrait, such as the boy reading down below. He was Vincenzo Foppa's idea of the young Cicero – Marcus Tullius Cicero, Roman philosopher, orator, letter writer, whom men almost worshipped in fifteenth-century Italy, when they were rediscovering the civilization of Rome: he seemed the model of virtue in law, in government, in living, and the model of perfect writing. Foppa makes him the perfect schoolboy (which he was, according to his biography). His problem was to picture a small boy, solid and solemn, but still a boy, who could be supposed to have become the Roman everyone so admired. He painted him, in this piece of fresco, on the walls of a bank. Not quite the modern bank around the corner, but the Milan bank of the Medici family, financiers, princes, scholars, patrons of art: you went in to talk business, and there was Cicero: talk your business as gravely and clearly as he would have done.

The 'real' boy in blue hat and red doublet is by another Italian, Pintoricchio – 'real' boy, in a 'real' landscape having his own thoughts and feelings expressed in these eyes, that obstinate mouth and chin, and the turn-up of his hat.

CICERO READING
Vincenzo Foppa
(1427/30–1515/16)

Portraits again. Different artists being true to different selves. The grand German lady, with her cold face and seven gold necklaces, was painted in 1564 by Lukas Cranach the Younger, much in the way his father (pages 30, 31) had painted. He's not cheating, and I expect this painter and subject were agreed, that this cold beauty wanted an accurate picture of herself, as a Somebody, who was never going to let that tied-together face smile at a mere you or me or a Lukas Cranach; whereas the other face, of the Algerian girl, painted in Paris some fifty years ago (this time the picture is more face than necklace), tells us much about the girl, and much more about the painter, Amedeo Modigliani –

PORTRAIT OF A WOMAN
Lukas Cranach the Younger
(1515 – 1586)

not the sad facts about him (that he was poor, ill, and unsuccessful, and given
to drink and drugs, dying young in a Paris hospital for the destitute); but the
good facts, that he lived to draw, to take the simplest curving lines of someone's
face and neck (it was usually a girl) and fill them with that person's life in a way
which made the picture equally *him*.

A great French painter, Nicolas Poussin, hundreds of years before Modigliani
was working, insisted that in good pictures there is something which comes
from the painter himself and which cannot be learned. He said it was like the
Golden Bough which Aeneas was destined to find in Virgil's poem the Aeneid —
the mistletoe bough of gold which led Aeneas safely into Hades and back to
Earth: it is something no one can find or pick unless he is led to it by fate. And
this is the something which tells us that pictures are by a certain painter, and
which gives us our pleasure, or most of it, when we look at them.

At Angers in France stands one of the strongest and most grim and growling of castles. Huge towers, black and white and walls like precipices go down and down into the moat. Inside once lived King René, King of Sicily, King of Naples, King of Jerusalem, Count of Provence, Duke of Lorraine and Duke of Anjou, a king who was a poet.

This King René of Anjou (which is the country round Angers) had to do plenty of fighting, but he preferred less royal pursuits. He liked nature and poetry and songs about love and dawn and May and romances about perfect knights and ladies of beauty and virtue. He liked to stage tournaments, to dress himself and his courtiers up, say, as shepherds. He liked to have round him poets and painters, as well as scholars who could tell them in France about all the new learning of Italy.

One thing he wrote (in 1457) was a romance about a good knight (really it was about himself and his dreams) he called Cuer–Sir Coeur, Sir Heart, as you might say, and how he travels with his aide and comrade Desire to rescue his lady Doulce Mercy, Gentle Favour, Gentle Mercy, who is held prisoner in the castle of Sir Dangier–Sir Hurtful, Sir Dangerous.

One of René's scribes wrote out his story of Sir Heart on leaves of vellum, one of his artists–we don't know his name, he is called simply the Master of King René–surrounded the story with borders of bright flowers, and added seventeen pictures of all that happened to Sir Heart and Desire on their dangerous journey.

Here, across the page, you see what happens at the very beginning. Sir Heart lies asleep in his curtained bed, and the winged god of love takes the red heart out of his breast and hands it over to Desire. Soon they will be off to the Dwarf Jealousy, and through the Forest, and to the Magic Well, and over the Plain, and to prison, and to the Island of Love.

If you go to King René's castle at Angers you will find there are many things there to contradict its sternness, and remind you of the gentleness of the king. Deer wander down in the moat, there is a garden of flowers along the broken battlements, and most beautiful great tapestries are hung in the rooms of the castle. In the green wood, the forest, outside Angers, King René when he was out hunting one day encountered a hermit. He built the hermit a cell, and built for himself, alongside, a retreat, a hermitage royal, a summer-house where he could talk art and poetry and romance. Perhaps it was there that René of Anjou talked over the dreamily lit illustrations with his master painter.

In the days of King René and his painter, there lived a greater artist, Jean Fouquet. Turn the page, and you will find something he painted to go in a prayer-book for a grandee of France, the king of France's rich treasurer, Étienne Chevalier.

THE GOD OF LOVE TAKES
POSSESSION OF THE
KNIGHT'S HEART
Master of King René of Anjou
(mid fifteenth century)

Ne nupt en ce mois passe
Trauaille tourmente lasse
Forment penses ou lit me mis
Comme homme las qui A si mis
Son cueur en la mercy damours
Que ma vie en plains et en plours

Shapes are put together which hardly look like a story, only a landscape round
a castle to which some horsemen are riding and where some girls are spinning
among the sheep. Here is what a new castle and girls and people on horses
looked like in France 500 years ago. Story it is, all the same. That girl on the
right standing up and holding her distaff and spinning—she has a halo round
her head. And that first horseman, though the party was riding to the castle,
has turned towards the girl.

She is St Margaret, innocent, fifteen years old; living, so legend says, not in
France about 1460, but long ago in Antioch. The horseman who has seen
Margaret, is wicked Olybius. He has fallen in love with her (and when she re-
fused him, and said she was a Christian, he had her tortured and then beheaded).
Her legend does tell that Olybius met St Margaret among the maidens and the
sheep. But when Étienne Chevalier looked at this picture in his prayer-book,
I think he would have supposed that, in a way, the sheep as well were, or had
been, demons (one *is* a black sheep)—because by legend St Margaret made
demons as tame as lambs.

Another saint of ancient times, St Anthony, with his pig. Where did St Anthony
live, and when? In fact in the Egyptian desert, more than eleven hundred years
before Hieronymus Bosch painted him. And you see where Hieronymus
Bosch sits him down, on a bank, not in Egypt but his own Holland. In monk's
clothing St Anthony finds what shelter he can, half in a hollow tree, under a bit
of extra roof of straw or reeds. His back is turned to the kind of country
Hieronymus Bosch saw every day, trees, fields, gates, hedges, bridges, dykes,
canals, church spires. He is not looking. He is not noticing the odd sharp
demons around—as extremely odd as demons might well be (and Bosch was

a painter who made things extra peculiar whenever he could—such as that building behind St Anthony which ends in a helmet). Back to the world, our world, the world of Hieronymus Bosch in 1490, St Anthony is refusing to be tempted, or to be upset.

In the desert, as Hieronymus Bosch knew, the Devil was said to have come to him in shapes small and enormous. Demons whacked him. Demons crawled to him looking like fabulous beasts. 'One howled, another siffled, and another cried, and another brayed and assailed St Anthony, that one with the horns, the others with their teeth, and the others with their paws and ongles, and disturned and all to-rent his body that he supposed well to die.'

What about the pig? Everyone knew a picture of St Anthony by his pig. In the Middle Ages it was supposed that Anthony had for companion in the desert only—well, not a pigsty pig, but a wild boar.

About 1500, some ten years after Hieronymus Bosch devised this Dutch St Anthony, stories from the Saint's life were painted on the back of oaken stalls in the cathedral at Carlisle, in England. On one of them this is how his pig is explained:

*Thys levyth he in wilderness XXIV yer and more*
*Without any company but the wilde boore.*

Watch a small naked soul being ferried by Charon across the Styx to the mouth of Hades. The sour ferryman is bringing the soul to a dominion of flame and darkness, to the mouth of Hades. But what is happening on the left? On the left to be seen more clearly in the colour detail, are the Elysian Fields. Most of the dead, the Greeks and Romans believed, were ferried over the Styx to the Infernal Regions. Particular heroes, including patriots and poets, were more lucky. They went to the Elysian Fields or the Isles of the Blest. That is the realm of light and flowers, on the left. Joachim Patenier has mixed a flavour of Heaven and Hell into his picture of the Elysian Fields, Charon, Styx and Hades. On the dark shore there are demons. On the Elysian side, where it is always spring and flowers are always out and birds are always singing, the happy ones are walking round with angels, and there is a heavenly palace there made of crystal.

THE PASSAGE OF THE
STYGIAN FLOOD (detail)
Joachim Patenier (died c1524)

How men worried and worried in the Middle Ages, in the centuries when our churches and cathedrals and castles were new, about what was going to happen to them after their death! Artists were always being asked for pictures of the dead rising out of their tombs or their graves at the sounding of the Last Trump, pictures of the Last Judgement before Christ on his throne which was often in the likeness of a rainbow, pictures of the souls being weighed by St Michael, Provost of Heaven, to test the good and the bad in their lives on earth, pictures of the separation of the Elect, whom angels guide into Heaven (remember the Elysian Fields a page back), from the Damned whom devils fork into Hell fire.

Holy Ghost Master
(early 15th century)

Men have never forgotten a splendid poem in Latin, the *Dies Irae*, which an Italian friar, Thomas of Celano, wrote seven centuries ago about this Last Day—

> *Day of Anger that shall turn*
> *The world to cinder*

—the day

> *When the trump shall hurl around*
> *The world's graves its wonder-sound*
> *Driving all men to the throne.*

In the Hungarian picture on the left, and in the small French painting out of a prayer-book, you see how the dead obey when the trumpets are blown. They break out of the ground, they push up their coffin lids. Everyone is suddenly reclothed with flesh and hair, though naked. There are no babies, no old people, only women and men. Everyone, you will notice, is about the same age—thirty years old. Christ was thirty years old when he rose from the dead, so it was held that when the graves opened and they came out of the ground, naked and bewildered by the light, they would all take on the resurrection age of Christ.

Here are the Egyptians caught in the Red Sea—soldiers, horses, chariots, waggons, an elephant with a howdah on its back—as they pursue the Israelites. The water had divided and rolled back, you will remember, when the Israelites passed over between a wall of Red Sea on either side. When the Egyptians came after them, the Lord slowed them down by making their chariot wheels come off—'And Moses stretched forth his hand over the sea, and the sea returned to his strength when the morning appeared . . . and the waters returned, and covered the chariots, and the horsemen, and all the host of Pharaoh that came into the sea after them; there remained not so much as one of them.'

In this charming fresco the drowning soldiers of Pharaoh don't look upset, and the sea doesn't look very deep or dangerous, though some of them are head down in the water with their feet sticking in the air. The painter was that gentle easy-going Bernardino Luini, the Italian who painted the girls bathing (page 26) along the wall of a summer villa in Milan. Round another of the rooms he painted frescoes—this one included—of the Story of Moses.

If the host of Pharaoh are no more worried than those girls, that was the way Luini painted, making everything into quiet shapes, quiet colours, hardly moving.

THE PASSAGE OF
THE RED SEA
Bernardino Luini
(c1481/2 – 1532)

MARTYRDOM OF ST JULIET
Catalan School (c1100)

A saint and martyr ('martyr' comes from a Greek word meaning a witness—to
Christianity) being sawn in two. Many churches were placed under the double
care of St Cyricus and his mother Julitta—the saint you owe your name to if
you are called Juliet, the saint Romeo's Juliet owed her name to. According to
their legend Juliet was killed, because she was a Christian, by the Roman
governor of Tarsus. First, while his men were beating her with raw sinews, her
little boy Cyricus scratched and bit this Roman governor. The governor threw
him down on the step and split his head open to the bone. Juliet persisted in
refusing to sacrifice to pagan gods, whereupon the governor had her skinned and
scalded with hot pitch and beheaded. Then she was cut in bits and scattered.

The artist who had to decorate an altar in honour of St Juliet and St Cyricus
(for a church in Catalonia, about 1100) painted two people sawing a woman
in two, as if she was a log on end—just that, in a straightforward way, to remind
people who came to her altar of what her end had been.

Opposite is the bible story of David and Goliath, painted, but how differently,
by Caravaggio, five hundred years later. Caravaggio was an artist who brawled,
drank and murdered; and died at 37 after giving a new energy to painting.
He brawled, too, with old ideas of art. Everything must be as it is, a saint must
not be in fancy dress. When he painted David and Goliath, David had to be
more 'real' than, say, Pintoricchio's boy (page 33), in a 'real' savage situation,
appearing sharply out of the dark with a 'real' sword, having cut off as 'real' a
head as any executioner—and on the real head he painted his own real features:
Goliath with the face of wild Caravaggio.

DAVID
Caravaggio (1573—1610)

46

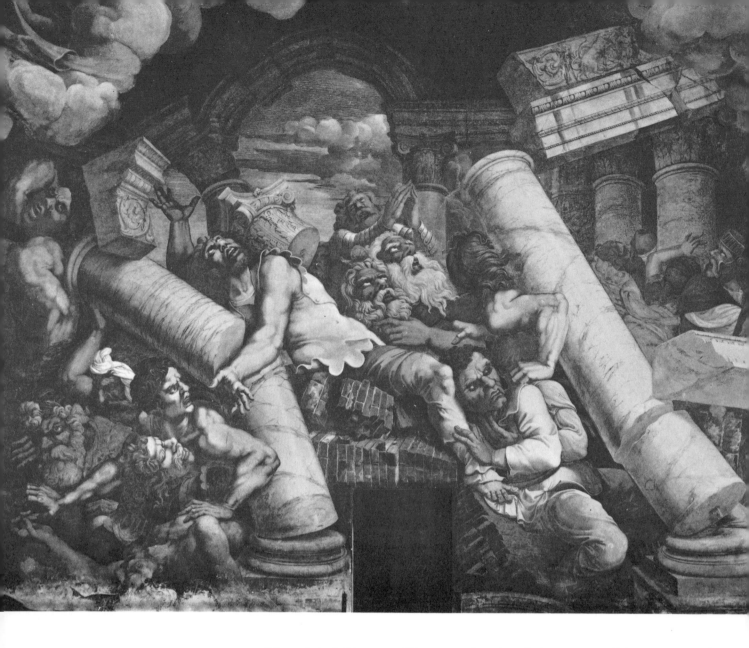

The original Giants or Gigantes, who give their name to all huge men, real or imaginary, were powerful, long haired, long bearded monsters of huge bulk. Their mother was Earth or Gaia, the earth-goddess, their father was the hell-god Tartarus; and they planned to climb into heaven and conquer the Olympian gods.

To get to heaven they pulled up mountains and loaded them on top of each other. On Olympus, which is the highest mountain in Greece (9573 feet above the sea), they piled Mt Ossa (6500 ft), on which they piled Mt Pelion (5300 ft); and there they were, on a level with the gods. They attacked them with rocks and burning trees, but were defeated at last. Pan terrified the Giants, put panic into them, by blowing his horn. Hercules, half earth born himself, though his father was Jupiter, shot giant after giant with his arrows, and Jupiter, Father of the Gods, threw them down, down and down with thunder and lightning, or with his thunderbolts.

The giants tumbled, mountains tumbled on them, their ammunition tumbled on them, the pillars and roofs of their own palaces tumbled on them, till

'. . . *Whelmèd in their wicked work these cursed Caitives lay.*'

The Giants came into the plans of Giulio Romano, architect and court painter to the Duke of Mantua, in 1524, when he designed a summer palace for his master in a meadow outside the city walls. He thought of having one room

painted by his assistants with the gentle story of how Cupid fell in love with Psyche, and another with all the violence of the violent tale of the Giants.

You go in – because this summer palace, the Palazzo del Tè, is still there – and Giants are being crushed all round you. You look up. There are the Gods among their Olympian clouds, most of them scared in a helter skelter way by the proceedings, though Jupiter and Juno are busy with thunderbolts.

Giulio Romano's idea was that walls, doors, windows, giants, rocks, columns seemed tumbling or caving in all round. Vasari, when he came to write about Giulio Romano, was delighted with the illusion of collapse. 'Between the tumbling walls there is a hearth, and when the fire is lighted the Giants seem to be burning.'

Legend put the war of the Gods against the Giants in various places, including the Phlegraean Fields in the volcano region just outside Naples, where hot springs have a sulphur smell, and sulphur fumes come sneaking out of the ground. Hercules, it is said, drove the Giants to these Phlegraean Fields. They washed their wounds, which gave the springs 'the tincture of sulphur . . . from the nature of the thunder which had struck them'.

The Gods pinned the Giants down in the Underworld. One is buried under Mt Etna. The huge chunk of rock which Athene threw at another Giant and which lies on him still, is the island we know as Sicily.

THE FALL OF THE GIANTS
Giulio Romano (c1499–1546)
and Rinaldo Mantovano

49

Do you remember in *Gulliver's Travels*, by Jonathan Swift, how Gulliver gets ashore after being wrecked, goes to sleep on the soft grass, sleeps extra well from tiredness, heat and half a pint of brandy he had drunk before leaving the ship, and then wakes up to find himself pegged down by the Lilliputians? Also how the Lilliputians loose arrows at him, and climb up him by ladders?

Perhaps Jonathan Swift had the idea from the obscure story — once well known in medieval romance — of how the legendary Pygmies tied Hercules down when he was asleep.

Gulliver's Lilliputians were only six inches tall. Lukas Cranach the Younger, when he painted the story, makes a Pygmy roughly what he should be by Greek and Roman legend, a little man one *pugme* high. Like a cubit in English, a *pugme* in Greek was the length of a normal man's forearm, or slightly more, $13\frac{1}{2}$ inches, elbow to knuckles. Cranach's pygmies, smaller at a cubit than any real dwarf, or real African pygmy, swarm round Hercules who is still asleep, there is an arrow in his beard, and one of them tries to get a better look at him from up a ladder. Their littleness emphasizes his bigness.

But what do you make of the giant by Goya, the greatest artist of Spain? He is Goya's own giant, I would say, not a story giant, sitting there on the world, on our world, above hills, rivers, villages. The night is going away with the waning moon: the sun is coming up, not visible yet, though it begins to light the giant's back and his face.

HERCULES AND THE PYGMIES
Lukas Cranach the Younger
(1515 – 1586)

I think the giant is *us*, the human race, our power—and our clumsiness. Sitting on the world and having a rest, is he a great bully who has been frightening everyone, and killing and wounding? Is the giant turning away from the moon and the night, which is a bad time, and noticing the daylight, coming after all, and puzzling him, huge monster, with a promise of good possibilities he doesn't quite understand? I believe so.

THE GIANT
Francisco de Goya y Lucientes
(1746–1828)

51

Many, many things, notions, names, we inherit from Greece and Rome. One of them is the name and notion of the Muses, nine goddesses, young and graceful, who breathe the arts into men.

Hesiod, Greek poet writing 2600 years ago, tells us in his poem *The Theogony* ('The birth of the Gods') about the Muses on Helicon, their holy mountain, walking and singing in the night, veiling themselves in mist, moving to shining dancing places, and breathing into poets a power to make songs so that we forget the things which worry us. He says the Muses gave him a branch of olive, and so made him a poet, when he was a poor shepherd lambing on Helicon. If you can, read Hesiod on the Muses, which helps us to understand about poetry and music (short for *mousike tekne*, the Muse's art)—and painting. Read him in the clear English of the translation by the American poet Richard Lattimore, whose *Hesiod* could—or should be—in the public library you go to. Or meanwhile you could read Matthew Arnold writing about the Muses singing and walking on Helicon, their breath sweeter than the wild thyme:

*They bathe on their mountain,*
*In the spring by their road;*
*Then on to Olympus*
*Their endless abode.*

*—Whose praise do they mention?*
*Of what is it told?*
*What will be for ever;*
*What was from of old.*

*First hymn they the Father*
*Of all things; and then,*
*The rest of immortals,*
*The action of men.*

*The day in his hotness,*
*The strife with the palm;*
*The night in her silence,*
*The stars in their calm.*

Now look at the picture—by Henri Rousseau (page 9)—*The Muse Inspiring the Poet*, inspiring Guillaume Apollinaire. The Muse hasn't stepped from Helicon, but is the girl Apollinaire loved, in Paris, the painter Marie Laurencin. Often a woman loved by a poet was spoken of as his Muse: love for her made him write, so she was his inspiration, like the goddesses.

Marie Laurencin wasn't pretty. But there she is, blue flower in her hair, saying 'Write!' There's Apollinaire with a quill pen. In front Rousseau has set a row of Sweet Williams, because in French they are *Oeillets de poète*.

Apollinaire was the poet who wrote (page 8) that a bird on an angel's shoulder and the angel sang together of Rousseau, and that Rousseau *was* both the bird and the angel.

THE MUSE INSPIRING
THE POET
Henri Rousseau (1844–1910)

A POET LOOKING AT
THE MOON (left)
Detail from
A POET DRINKING TO
THE MOON (right)
Ma Yüan (flourished
*c*1190−1224)

Hesiod put poets next to wise and good governors. Nizami the Persian poet (page 24) said that in Paradise there stand before God, first the prophets, then the poets. The Chinese, longest civilized of the peoples of the world, always respected them greatly, and their painters often set in their landscapes a poet contemplating nature, and often read poems to give themselves the mood for seeing nature, especially mountains, all pleasurable and quiet in front of them.

Poets or philosophers gaze at nature in these two pictures, on silk, which were painted by Ma Yüan, Painter in Attendance at the court of one of the emperors of China during the thirteenth century. They are in the mountains. One of them gazes up at the moon, his servant standing on one side and not interrupting. The other is so overcome, is feeling so much one and for ever with nature that he is making himself as rapt as possible by drinking – to the moon, which you cannot see because I've included only half the painting – his servant holding the wine. Each of them could say what one Chinese poet of the twelfth century said – that having finished reading books for a while, he was now reading mountains.

Ancient Chinese painters observed rules which they thought would help them to find and enter the true spirit of a scene. One master, Kuo Hsi, in *The Great Message of Forests and Streams*, said that in a mountain scene, you should look first for the 'master peak', and arrange everything else accordingly. Then when you came to rocks and trees, he said that you must first think about a large old pine, which could be called 'the aged master'. The aged master, like a man of virtue to lesser men, would help you to decide on the smaller details such as stones and plants, and help you to arrange them. Each of these pictures has its 'aged master'. And from the 'aged master', in the left hand picture, three pine-needles joined together are falling in the stillness.

Isn't it strange that this great poet of ancient China and this great poet of modern Europe should look so much alike, each with a hanging moustache and a small beard stuck on his chin?

The modern poet is Rainer Maria Rilke, of Germany, painted by Paula Modersohn-Becker, his friend; whereas the Chinese poet is an imaginary portrait of a real poet, T'ao Ch'ien, painted in 1650, one thousand two hundred and twenty-three years after his death by a Chinese master Ch'en Hung-shou, who liked to remember the painters and poets of the past.

He sits his poet down on a palm leaf in front of a rock. T'ao is meditating. His eyes are shut and a small wind is moving his beard. I think you must imagine him facing a landscape, or white clouds.

At any rate he is alone. Perhaps he's meditating—as he often does in his poems—on how all things pass away and how we should enjoy the present. On the rock are his two fans, also his brush, his ink-stick, his ink-tray and a dish of water, so he can write when he opens his eyes again.

Thinking of the sun and moon T'ao Ch'ien said in one poem 'When *we* go down, we never shine again'. In another poem about a clear cold morning on 9 October, in AD 409, he wrote:

*I do not know*
*    about a thousand years*
*Rather let me make*
*    this morning last for ever.*

If we didn't know, I am not sure we would guess from his portrait that Rilke was a poet and not the mysterious villain of a spy story. Does his portrait

THE POET T'AO CH'IEN
MEDITATING (detail from a scroll
Ch'en Hung-shou (1599–1652)

give a clue to his poems? T'ao Ch'ien buried himself in the country, Rilke buried himself in great cities (and in the castles of rich princesses who admired him). But this large-eyed man with red eyelids could look and look at something, let us say, a gazelle or a blue hydrangea, then lead it or lift it into a poem; there it seems to live, as if enclosed in glass, more entirely seen than ever before. And this Chinese poet, who probably did look as strange as Ch'en Hung-shou makes him, preserves for us evenings with a full moon, or willows looking white in frost, or the green face of Chinese wine.

Let us look for a contact between them. Rilke once wrote, of a girl he loved, that he and she were the two strings of a viol, and that a player's bow drew from the two of them a single voice:

*On what instrument are we two spanned?*
*What player holds us in his hand?*
*O sweet, sweet song.*

T'ao Ch'ien was fond of a lute which had no strings at all—fond of handling it. Friends would come and see him in his country home, they would drink wine, they would ask him why he was so fond of this lute without strings. He would reply that the music was inside the lute; which was all he cared about—'Why bother about the notes and the strings?'

The men in white hats? They are pilgrims in Japan, in a print by the great master Hokusai (drawn by himself on pages 11 and 12), coming down the sacred volcano, Mt Fuji, after paying their respects on top to the mountain-gods. The pilgrims are on a slope of volcanic cinders. Each has the same two characters on his hat—Chinese characters saying Fu-ji, which means 'no two'— not another mountain like Fuji, without equal. This is a woodcut from Hokusai's *One Hundred Views of Fuji*. (Turn two pages; and there is the Peerless Mountain again, in winter.)

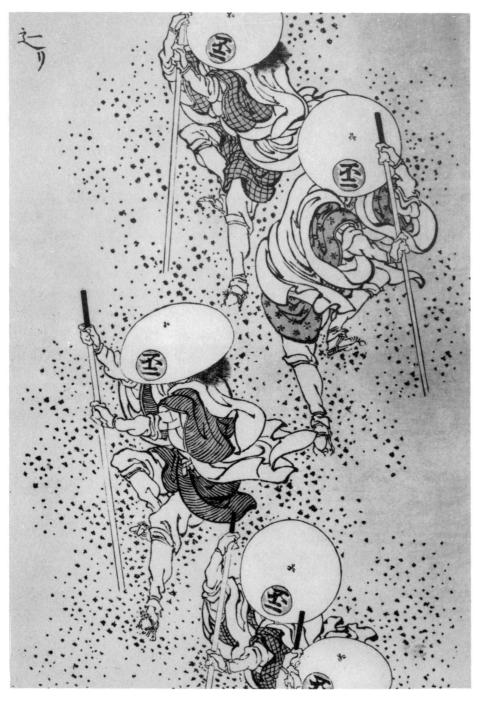

THE DESCENT FROM FUJI
Hokusai (1760—1849)

DANTE IN THE WOOD
Jacopo Ligozzi (1547–1626)

Journeys, pilgrimages—and another poet: shapes of people moving through the shapes of the world. The poet is Dante, one of the grandest poets of mankind (who lived from 1265 to 1321), at the very beginning of his poem *La Divina Commedia*, the beginning of his poem journey which is to take him through Hell, Purgatory and Paradise.

*Nel mezzo del cammin di nostra vita*
  *mi ritrovai per una selva oscura,*
  *che la diritta via era smarrita.*

Say those lines to yourself aloud (even if you don't bother about the pronunciation); they are among the most famous lines ever written—

*In the middle of the journey of our life*
  *I found myself going through a gloomy wood*
  *In which I lost the rightness of my way.*

*Per una selva oscura*—the wood is tangled and difficult, but Dante says the first rays of the sun are shining through, and lessening his fear. In our drawing he is pictured, at dawn, by Jacopo Ligozzi, a painter who lived in Dante's Florence two centuries after his death. Artists, though, know what Dante looked like, since he had been painted by his friend Giotto in a fresco in a Florentine chapel.

59

It can be exciting going into a gallery for the first time and finding a picture you like and haven't seen before. Years ago I climbed the steps on a very hot day to see if there were things to enjoy in the art gallery at Tours, in France—and there was one of the great paintings, 'Christ in the Garden of Olives' by Mantegna. Below is the part of it I never forget—that road winding down from Mantegna's Jerusalem, people walking down behind soldiers and Judas: then, the rocks, the wooden bridge, the rabbit, the dead tree and its colony of bracket fungus.

CHRIST IN THE GARDEN
OF OLIVES (detail)
Andrea Mantegna (c1431 – 1506)

ASHIDA
Ando Hiroshige (1797–1858)

I try to see that picture again every summer. And once when I was looking
through an album of colour prints by the two Japanese artists Eisen and
Hiroshige, I looked at the curving road—this curving road (above) bordered
with a slope of green, by Hiroshige—remembered the bends of the road and
descending in Mantegna's picture, hundreds of years and thousands of miles
between them. Since then I have always thought of these two together.

Hiroshige's travellers are on the Kiso-kaido, the road through the mountains
from Kyoto, the old capital, where the mikado of Japan had his court, to Edo,
the Eastern Capital which became Tokyo. The album is called *The Sixty-nine
Stations of the Kiso-kaido*. In moonshine, mist, snow, sunshine, Hiroshige painted
the scenes around each stopping place along the several hundred miles of this
mountain highway, where horses could be exchanged, and travellers could pass
the night.

Over the page Hokusai's winter travellers pass Mt Fuji.

FUJI IN A SNOWSTORM
Hokusai (1760–1849)
*over page*

61

深雪の
不二

Here is a picture journey which might have been taking place—in China—before stiff William the Conqueror ever won the battle of Hastings. Through a gorge of rocks in wild country grooms and soldiers are escorting a tribute horse, led by a rein. It must have been a very special tribute horse. It is saddled, but the saddle is protected by a piece of silk embroidered with dragons. No one will be allowed on the back of this horse except the Emperor.

Barbarians who lived outside the Great Wall, in the steppes, would send tribute horses to the Emperors of China in this way, the horses making a long journey which wore their hooves thin. Two splendidly dressed barbarians ride at this horse's tail, carrying pennons, and themselves mounted on horses wearing feathery masks which give them the look of dragons.

In China dragons weren't shapes of the devil. They were divine majestic creatures living in storm-clouds, who gave people the rain of life. Horses were related to dragons: horses were dragons on earth, with dragon energy and dragon speed—and fine names, as a rule. The Emperor might ride on Running Rainbow or Drifting Cloud or Shining Light of the Night.

With his escort this Shining Light of the Night (which wouldn't be a bad name for a white horse like a summer cloud) was painted by an unknown artist of the Sung dynasty, perhaps a thousand years ago. He may have been recalling the gift of some famous and particularly dragon-like horse to one of the T'ang emperors 200 years before.

Detail from THE TRIBUTE
HORSE, painted c1000 AD by an
artist of the Sung dynasty

Our next two pictures over the page, are of people in a rare hurry on land, on sea; in war, in a regatta; in the mountains of China, and on the lagoon at Venice.

Like Europeans later on, the Chinese often painted scenes of the past recalling heroes or famous events. In the Sung dynasty (960–1279) one of the great painters was Chao Po-chü. Early in the twelfth century he painted a scroll imagining the triumph in 206 BC of Han Kao-tsu, the first Emperor of Han, and founder of China's greatest dynasty. Then in the sixteenth century, in the time of the Ming emperors, an artist painted a copy of Chao Po-chü's scroll;

which copy in our own century has come to rest in the museum at Boston, in New England. Here is part of it.

Han Kao-tsu was a farmer's son, the first humbly-born Chinese to become emperor. In 206 BC he finished off his rebellion against the second of the Ch'in emperors, last of a dynasty which had bent the backs of the Chinese with taxes and forced labour (it was the first Ch'in emperor who built the Great Wall of China, to keep out the barbarians).

Since the Han proved so grand and glorious a dynasty (the one in which Buddhism came to China), it was natural to imagine such a scene of its foundation; in the scroll you see the First Emperor's army winding uphill and downhill, over bridges, through gates, through gorges, round crags, between mountains, under clouds and pines, on their rapid way to occupy a last stronghold of the Ch'in forces. Or rather, for much of the way, you don't see them: you see only their pennons; you see they are cavalry, they are galloping, the lances lean forward, the pennons stream back with their speed.

So the scroll suggests power, purpose, triumph. As a matter of real history

Detail from ENTRY OF THE FIRST EMPEROR OF THE HAN DYNASTY INTO KUAN CHUNG, after Chao Po-chü (early 12th century)

66

Han Kao-tsu wasn't such a good soldier, though he won, and the old empire tumbled. But then he turned out to be a very clever ruler. He told his generals 'You know how to command soldiers. I know how to command generals.' He did, and the dynasty he founded lasted four centuries, from BC 206 to 220 AD.

The trick of painting an army by showing just a few lances is one which our painters have also used. I expect you will have seen reproductions of 'The Surrender of Breda', a famous picture by the Spanish master Velasquez (1599–1660). Not much army is visible, only seven soldiers and a general on the defeated side, and nine soldiers and a general on the winning side. But behind the nine soldiers 30 lances stand against the sky, and far away in a valley you can make out another 26 lances. Enough to suggest an army. This painting by Velasquez is often called 'Las Lanzas', the Lances.

The Chinese artist has painted, if my account is correct, 29 lances—no, 28 lances and one flag—in movement, in our part of his scroll. Then 17 lances, and one flag, standing up straight, at rest. Movement against rest. Attack and arrival. The First Emperor of Han has won.

The boats haring up, then down across the waves (below) are crossing the lagoon at Venice in what the Venetians were the first to call a regatta, a boat race (you can see the word $^{REGA}_{TA}$ obligingly inscribed down at the bottom). I have taken this race from one corner of a huge woodcut of all Venice, lagoon, canals, buildings, and snowy Alps in the background, and winds blowing at the four corners. It was made, I expect to sell to tourists in Venice, by the artist known as Jacopo de' Barbari, in 1500. This name means Jacob of the Barbarians, which seems to have been a rather impolite way of saying that he wasn't a Venetian, but a German. But then in 1500 Venice was the richest and most cultured city of Europe, altogether—and rightly—pleased with itself.

The boats are pressing forward like Han Kao-tsu's cavalry. The oars (and the oarsmen) lean forward like the Chinese lances; and all those little triangles which indicate the waves, lean forward too and chase each other, in the same direction. Often you can find pictures inside pictures in this way.

Detail from woodcut of VENICE
Jacopo de' Barbari
(c1440/50–c1516)

67

Venice and regattas—that Venetian word *regata* or *regatta* meant first of all something squabbled over, a squabbling, a noisy wrangling such as salesmen make when they are shouting against each other in a street market; then it meant the kind of noisy wrangling to be heard from boatmen shouting against each other in Venetian dialect, in a race; then it meant the race itself; last of all it came to mean—as we use regatta in English, Henley Regatta and so on—a whole day or festival of races.

Everyone went to Venice to see festivities ashore and afloat, the grandest in the world, on the lagoon or on the Grand Canal, which was, and remains, the grandest 'street' in the world; which brings me to the boat of gold, on the opposite page. It is the Bucintoro, painted by the Venetian artist Francesco Guardi.

Once a year, on Ascension Day, the Doge (i.e. the Duke) of Venice was rowed in this wonderful barge out to the open sea near the entrance into the lagoon. There he renewed the marriage between the sea and the Republic of Venice, whose ships ruled the Adriatic and most of the Mediterranean.

The Bucintoro looked like gold right down to the water. It was spiky with statues and carvings covered with gold leaf, golden tritons, golden mermaids, golden shells, golden Muses and Virtues, golden cheeks which spouted a fair wind, golden Syrens with outstretched wings whose breasts touched the small waves of the lagoon or the Adriatic.

The Doge sat in a cabin of state towards the golden beak, on a throne from which he could contemplate the figure of gold which shows there in the picture above the blue water—Time, with his scythe and his hour-glass. All things pass away. Even Doges—and even, as it turned out, the Bucintoro and the Republic of Venice.

St Mark, the saint who cared for Venice—or rather the winged lion which is his symbol—is there curling a gold paw over the very end of the beak, in front of the golden figures of Justice and Peace. Twenty-four long red oars on each flaming side drove this vision of a boat, silver trumpets sounding, and then a choir of trebles singing, across a lagoon sprinkled with gondolas, past the Lido, the long island which shelters the lagoon, and into the open Adriatic; where the Doge threw into the sea a golden wedding ring which had been blessed by the Patriarch of Venice.

As he did so he said in Latin *Desponsamus te, Mare, in signum veri perpetuique domini.*

We wed thee, Ocean, in sign of true and everlasting dominion.

Perhaps he should have touched wood, because the dominion wasn't everlasting. In 1797, only four years after the death of Francesco Guardi, who had seen so many Ascension Days, Napoleon captured Venice, put an end to the Venetian Republic, and had the Bucintoro hacked of its golden decorations. They were piled up and burnt. Napoleon wanted the gold, from all that gold leaf.

Detail from THE DEPARTURE
OF THE BUCINTORO FOR
ST NICHOLAS DI LIDO
Francesco Guardi (1712 – 1793)

In our picture the Doge and the Bucintoro are just leaving for this annual wedding of the Sea.

After bringing the Doge back to his palace of pink marble, the Bucintoro would have been rowed off into the Arsenal ('arsenal', for a government arms factory and arms store, is another word we have borrowed from the Venetians) and carefully put away under linen wrapping until the next Ascension Day.

Once, in 1620, an English merchant came to Venice, and greatly admired the Bucintoro as it moved out to the wedding; but no, he could not believe that the Doges threw the gold wedding ring into the sea. He swore they tied it to a piece of string, lowered it into the Adriatic, and drew it up again—as if a gold ring a year would have made any difference to the wealth of Europe's wealthiest city. I fear that merchant had rather a mean business mind.

VENICE, from a manuscript of
Marco Polo's *Li Livres du Graunt
Caam*, c 1 400

The picture on this page shows how Venice looked to an English or at any
rate a northern artist about the year 1400. There is the Grand Canal opening on
the left, there are the bridges over lesser canals, and other things still to be seen
in Venice, particularly the two pillars, on one of them the Lion of St Mark, on
the other St Theodore killing a crocodile, and beyond them the palace of the
Doges, and beyond that again the great church of St Mark, built nine centuries
ago, topped with four bronze horses which were once in Nero's Rome and then
in Constantine's Constantinople.

I like those two swans, head and neck under water, white ends in the air. The
painter had noticed how swans swivel round in that way, as they look for food.

Out on its low islands, so full of light from the sky all round, and light reflected from the canals, Venice became for 300 years the home of great artists, rather than great poets or writers (though one Venetian poet did write that Rome was built by men, and Venice by gods).

Carpaccio, Bellini, Giorgione, Titian, Tintoretto, Paolo Veronese, Piazzetta, Tiepolo, Canaletto, Francesco Guardi, whose picture of the Bucintoro we have been looking at – they are some of that marvellous company of keen-eyed artists, between 1460 and 1780, who have left us many of the masterpieces of all time.

One of the noblest of them, Tintoretto – he lived from 1518 to 1594 – said something about being a painter which is worth remembering. Yes, there were good colours for sale in the shops in Venice, but good painting could be extracted, he said, 'only from the jewel-box of a painter's talent with patient study and sleepless nights'. He added that few people understood good painting, and few were capable of it. So good pictures have always been treasured; and every national gallery owns pictures from Venice.

But for our last picture, let's go east, again – since pictures are made everywhere in the world – to Persia.

ALEXANDER AND THE TALKING TREE, from a manuscript of Firdawsi's *Shahnama, c1430* over page

Over the page stands Alexander the Great, Sikandar, as the Persians called him, and believe it or not, that tree is talking to him and telling him things he does not want to hear. Legends grew up about Alexander: he lived a life of magic and marvel, he flew through the air in a glass cage, he visited the floor of the sea in a glass bell, he built an iron wall across a pass in the Caucasus to keep out the giants Gog and Magog, he looked for the waters of the Well of Life in the Land of Gloom; and he found this Talking Tree.

This picture of Alexander and the Tree was made about 1430 for a new manuscript of Persia's most famous poem the *Shahnama*, by Persia's greatest poet Firdawsi. The *Shahnama*, finished in 999, is the epic of the Shahs of Persia; and one of them is Alexander, or Sikandar, who comes to a city where he is told of the marvel of a Tree which speaks, a Tree with two trunks. One trunk is male and speaks only in daytime, one is female and speaks, and gives out scent, only at midnight.

'What is beyond this Tree?' asks Alexander. 'Nothing', they tell him, 'the Tree grows at the End of the World.' He finds the branches covered with the heads of animals eaten by worshippers of the Tree. At midday the Tree gives a frightening and foreboding cry: the leaves of the male trunk rustle and tell him 'Soon you must lose your throne'. At midnight the leaves of the musk-scented female trunk tell him 'You have been greedy. You have caused affliction, you have brought death to kings. Soon you will die.' And Alexander (who died in Babylon) goes away, 'stricken in heart by the scimitar of fate'.

Since this Tree grows at the End of the World, you must imagine that if Alexander steps forward just a little he will step right over the world's edge into blue emptiness.